impact
statement

impact
statement

jody chan

Brick Books

Library and Archives Canada Cataloguing in Publication

Title: Impact statement / Jody Chan.
Names: Chan, Jody, author.
Identifiers: Canadiana (print) 20230583121 | Canadiana (ebook) 2023058313X | ISBN 9781771316255 (softcover) | ISBN 9781771316262 (EPUB) | ISBN 9781771316279 (PDF)
Subjects: LCGFT: Poetry.
Classification: LCC PS8605.H3549 I47 2024 | DDC C811/.6—dc23

We gratefully acknowledge the Canada Council for the Arts, the Government of Canada through the Canada Book Fund, and the Ontario Arts Council and the Government of Ontario for their support of our publishing program.

Edited by Mercedes Eng.

Cover image:
Rain
Jenny Chen
Mixed Media on Paper, 5.5 x 7.5 inches

Author photo by Sarah Bodri.
The book is set in PF Marlet Display and Arno Pro.
Design by Emma Allain.

Brick Books
487 King St. W.
Kingston, ON
K7L 2X7
www.brickbooks.ca

BRICK BOOKS

Though much of the work of Brick Books takes place on the ancestral lands of the Anishinaabeg, Haudenosaunee, Huron-Wendat, and Mississaugas of the Credit peoples, our editors, authors, and readers from many backgrounds are situated from coast to coast to coast in Canada on the traditional and unceded territories of over six hundred nations who have cared for Turtle Island from time immemorial. While living and working on these lands, we are committed to hearing and returning the rightful imaginative space to the poetries, songs, and stories that have been untold, under-told, wrongly told, and suppressed through colonization.

CONTENT NOTE

if you ever faced coercion or confinement instead of care

if ever defined and diminished by the state

if reading about violence: medical / carceral / psychiatric /
administrative / eugenic / intimate / institutional / systemic

evokes: shame / grief / rage / regret

please take: care / space / risk / whatever you need
(I mean it)

if you ever forged: home / pleasure / hope for a future

from the ruins of textbook / ledger / occupation

from an archive in which you would not find your name

I am reaching for you

TABLE OF CONTENTS

the garden where our future grows ◆ 13

MEDICAL HISTORY

a guide to pronouns ◆ 23
patient record ◆ 25
pageantry ◆ 27
trauma time ◆ 29
intergenerational ◆ 30
the psychiatrist arrives late to my assessment ◆ 31
money model of madness ◆ 33
glossary ◆ 35
narrative therapy ◆ 37
content warning ◆ 38
CPTSD: emotional flashback ◆ 39
risk assessment ◆ 42
borderline personality disorder ◆ 43
    as the happiest I've ever been
    as personality test
    as logic puzzle
    as language-resistant
self-diagnosis between after and before ◆ 49

DIAGNOSIS

patient record: Velma Demerson ◆ 55
interview: Velma Demerson ◆ 57
the doctor seeks supporting evidence ◆ 58
interview: Velma Demerson ◆ 59

a note on mothers • 60

liability culture • 61

patient record: Marie "Blanche" Wittman • 63

etiology • 64

a note on white • 71

TREATMENT PLAN

triage • 75

abandonment issues • 76

management model of madness • 78

patient record: ghost chorus • 81

etymology • 82

a history of confinement, different sites • 85

a history of labour • 87

brick in the asylum wall, 1861 • 90

Parkdale time-lapse • 91

brick in the heritage wall, 2020 • 92

a note on absence • 93

in a single day, a world can end • 96

lately, I live in history • 98

PROGRESS NOTES

a note on presence • 104

quarantine • 106

possibility model of madness • 109

a note on mothers • 110

abolish • 113

longing is our connecting place • 114

IMPACT STATEMENT ✦ 117

a community witnesses ✦ 132
index ✦ 137
unhaunted ✦ 138
stage directions for a future garden ✦ 140

the researcher cites their sources ✦ 142
acknowledgments ✦ 146

Queer femme suicide is not a side note to the struggle.

— Leah Lakshmi Piepzna-Samarasinha,
from *Care Work: Dreaming Disability Justice*

Abolition is about presence, not absence.
It's about building life-affirming institutions.

— Ruth Wilson Gilmore

THE GARDEN WHERE OUR FUTURE GROWS

wanting to die transforms time and space, in that there is no longer a map.

that home is on the other side of leaving, that growing up
I folded into corners to not be seen.

to take the dog out, to sink, to bathe, to unclog the brain.
my father asks why I never visit anymore.
the tasks of basic survival begin to stretch out across weeks.

during an episode, I wander without shoes

or story, trying to explain myself

to myself. like falling in love, my impulse

to flight I've considered extravagant. weak.

the blast radius of suicidality is that the one in pain becomes
a scapegoat. I let the garbage ferment too long, found maggots
in the bin. of course I blamed myself.
even the house consumes its own light.

I swallow theory like it can save me. I can barely think
outside of writing, let alone feel. when my parents settled
here, they changed names between airports, as if to delete
a history. I afford rent on the rooms I live in. this land is not
my home. the words I have for this are always changing.
like dictionary entries, I gather longing. *ancestor*: a deficit
mentality. *aftermath*: the moment I realize I have travelled
in the wrong direction for hours. I memorize, repeat.
by the time I meet the psychiatrist, I have tried to die
twice. my existence is an accident of accumulation. every verse
I compose, an evidence against me. I don't know
if two is too many, so I don't ask. nothing is settled in me.
not the way the line breaks, not the half-life of grief.

Dreaming otherwise is as essential as food for us to survive.

who swim nude in the river in September
who sweat the eggplant overnight
who amass inhalers, benzos, anti-psychotics to share
who goodbye their grandparent over Zoom
who know the hotline numbers, and which ones call the cops
who populate the Google doc, consider
    meeting agendas a commitment to the future
who beg prescription refills, who bleed
    for tests many times a month
who know not to hospitalize
by default, who believe the days
ahead of me, who drive
       out to Tommy Thompson, gather rocks
  for grounding, we stumbled on two cottontails
     that day, the shadow of geese
   nearly tangling underfoot
     who tether me, mother
     me, from breath to breath
when I lose time
 when I don't know that I am
who offer guest room, groceries, their palms
  to touch, who nourish
the conditions for dreaming
  knowing someday the time for dreaming will be

a radical kinship, an interdependent sociality, a politics of care

contradictions in suicide intervention:

it is not revolutionary to overrule
another's bodily autonomy.
it is not revolutionary to let someone die
neglected by the systems we live in.
hiding your pain can kill you.
being perceived as too much can kill you.
it is okay to feel
everything. it is okay
not to feel.
I am afraid of death.
I am not afraid to die.
a supporter knows nothing.
a supporter has a demand.
a demand requires a target.
a target requires movement, hands
            stirring dirt before
            dirt turns identifiably garden.
you cannot move past the grief; the grief must move
            through you.
the grief must sting, settle, sediment, sunder, before it can
mother you.
no one can save you but yourself.
it is not your responsibility to save anyone.
it is not revolutionary to let yourself die.

If grief can be the garden. If femme suicide and death can be loss, and can also be a sign pointing to what needs to change.

in the quiet season, there are questions to confront. a safety plan requires the discipline to dream. for a time, I could not be left alone with pen or pill. I declared my mouth a cemetery, taped emergency contacts to the fridge. then I named myself anew. then gathered the years, the beds of dirt, then knew. I was not ready to be an ancestor. *my grief about femme suicide is the garden where our future grows.* our task, merely, is to make possible. to uproot the flags. to revise the old dictionaries. finally, I can admit: I dream of care
that has nothing to do with survival.

MEDICAL HISTORY

A GUIDE TO PRONOUNS

I :: I

I :: patient, denied, enduring

I :: future ancestor

I :: ghost chorus

I :: an instance of *we*

I :: the evidence of *you*

we :: what *they* turn away from

they :: victim :: oppressor :: bystander :: border

they :: my name in your mouth

we :: an attempt

an ancillary function of the institution :: as in, *we*
  acknowledge what

harm *we* have done :: so let us fling the past :: in the wind

we, then :: an illusion :: a marketing strategy

 and yet :: this is *your* history :: *my* tilted ice

our :: a screen tinted red at night

I :: researcher :: regarding *you* safely

through the window of the page

PATIENT RECORD

MEDICAL HISTORY:

youngest of the family, by flights and decades. never pregnant, might
want to be. sleep as needed, or four hours daily. extra dopamine if
the doctor will prescribe it. mother, mother's mother, and her mother
before that— died young, by multiple causes. by melancholic mood. by
flooded lung. by rivers exceeding their banks. by trading one colony for
another. everyone has a story but no one talks.

DIAGNOSIS:

pills for nightmares, for pain. for rain in the joints, only partially
metabolized. content warning: vocabulary consisting mainly of
wounds and words for hunger. if letters of confirmation are required,
then these: BPD, CPTSD, peeled tangerines in one long strip. leave
an island city. leave the radio loud, all night. lineage littered with the
impulses of investment and industry. fill the home with this and that,
rocks, pinecones, dirty spoons. how we might give back what we took.
the land, at least. how we scavenged, always seeking for *we* to signify
something stable.

TREATMENT PLAN:

to straddle past and possible at once
to exist estranged
      from dreaming, from rage
to be decided upon
to be an I of many parts
to chart
      the hearth   the ward
      the administrator   the archive
      the barred   the locked
      the shuttered window the laddered heart

PAGEANTRY

the women I desire in my dreams are always
white. they wait like cutlery in

well-organized drawers, free of other
bodies— a spectacle of muscled

mares. theatre after theatre, the women's
white limbs dazzle in swimwear, sleek

as champion horses. the women more discerning than
the breeders—

white-gloved and disciplinary.
   I have this fantasy where I'm force-

fed what's best for me, plain porridge trickling
white-hot trails down my off-

white neck. in the dream I grid
   facts into a notebook until I

disappear inside its guiltless
white pages, as if to tumble down the throat

of a toilet or a glass hallway. until 2017
every Mr Gay World winner was

white. before 1930 every Hong Konger living above
   a specified altitude on Victoria Peak was also

white. I fall and fall. each way I turn, a scrawny
  foal collides with a mirror, the shock

whitening its breast.

TRAUMA TIME

her face stomps the world to a standstill. the third time we fall

away beside each other, I wake naming our children. I'm
trying not to skip ahead, only linger

here, a stranger's exhale on my forehead
my excuse to gaze at her sleeping chin

which somehow seems so kind, and today I am okay
even though I have been a strawberry beneath

a knife, a blade of grass beneath a cat's paw.
this could be different. we could compost

our lives before each other, grow
lilacs in fertile pots and come up

for air when our tongues cramp.
the morning becoming a banana split

open to reveal a fresh body. she
doesn't know me but maybe

if she would stay for breakfast or just stay
asleep I'd stop making plans

for the other side of death

INTERGENERATIONAL

mist gathers across
the lake like memory. my hair
unbraided sheds into the morning
coffee. violence taught me
to fear myself, sidewalks, ground
ivy, the lemon tree reaching over
my shadow. I long to embody my lineage
without shame, yet I static when she enters
the room. in the wartime stories, my mother
hides behind a crewcut. let the soldiers believe
she is a boy, her body an accumulation of sweet
potato skin and salt. she pretends the war
is over, as if there is only the one
that birthed her. she says I'm lucky
I can't be sick for the place she came from.
I was born here, backdrop of ponytails
and antidepressants. nobody ever rationed
my rice or claimed my schoolyard as killing
site. choosing this city means I cry
over mulberries, their sweetness spread
on gravel. when she left home, she left
my breath behind.

THE PSYCHIATRIST ARRIVES LATE TO MY ASSESSMENT

she asks me to rate my childhood from 1-10 as a conversation
starter— I answer too many of her questions

yes, my tone chipper, cardboard, clink clink
another big-T terrible

for the ACE machine— she explains
epigenetics, neurobiology, she's surprised by my

quote unquote *success*, how my trauma
means I'm just a first draft of the person

I could be— other people's lives
described to me as vivid, ornate—

if my dad had crafted with me after school
for example, straw necklaces, paper puppets

on the mantel, needle leaping on the record player, if
she could locate home video montage of me

and my best friends, dabbing funfetti
on each other's noses— she pities

me, wasted girl— carcass, carnation, something sweet
for time to spoil— here's the script, here's

the night tremor, dimmed impulse— her bangs
blunt, her decor blandly monochromatic, a mosquito

dead against my window— we're out of
minutes— there are many ways to avoid

meeting someone— a fence, a diagnostic
knell— I'm swallowing

myself in the camera— she
hasn't looked at me once

MONEY MODEL OF MADNESS

Care is not care until it is counted

Each filled bed, each head's turgid lake spilled
over the lip of a therapy hour

The renamed asylum hosts vaccine clinics, flower stands
jewellery-making classes

Over screens, a matrix of hands stringing beads onto stiff necklaces

Single-file lines suggest an intertwining structure
the accumulation of gestures

Sure, former patients polished the iron fences closing themselves in

Ten-foot boundary wall, double-bricked

The administrator calculates the relative cost
of warehouse and cure

The administrator exists to maximize return on investment

To shave down the distance between worker and surplus, between
revenue and body

Not to surrender a patient discharge form, nor a formal apology

It takes lifetimes to excise the locked ward from one's vocabulary

Each hallway lit like a microwave, sensation
of snowfall in the throat

Confinement takes place on a public-private continuum

All mothers take place on the other side of a latched door

POV: you're at the brain doctor's office again, confronted with a
Feelings Wheel— please select between Disgust, Déjà Vu, Arousal,
Apathy

The administrator's kink is productivity

Crushed velvet pillowcases, cardamom plum jam in little jars

Wrists bound to beds with lilac ribbons

Lobotomies tested on taxpayers in the lowest bracket

Across the live edge of a neighbouring alleyway, a mural cries
YOU'VE CHANGED

GLOSSARY

able-bodied

all your life, the phone never stops ringing.
the rich throw money at clocks.

psychiatric assessment

the police administrator says, *compliance can be best achieved through tactics of terror.*
the doctor says, *if you are at risk of hurting yourself or others we have to call the police.*

CPTSD

I lurch awake to sirens, heartbeat stumbling.
dream journal recorded in a language I can't read.

medical debt

a body worth only how it is numbered. the nursing home makes two hundred dollars per head, per day.

mandatory reporting

two women lock hands in a public space. I lied
about wanting to die to keep myself safe.

organized abandonment

mayor increases the police budget: fifty million.
medically assisted dying replaces food, healthcare, housing.

NARRATIVE THERAPY

swing set empty   whale-stickered window   soup congealed
no one spoke over   the television   he pursued me with
a feather duster   humour is what happens   when the truth
is impossible   the grocer casts meat after   meat onto
the scale   the mother in my head wants me   to be alone
she threw my brother   in a garbage can   *did I say you
could cry*   she approached me with the scissors   *did I say
you could stop   crying*   blood edged into   the bok choy
kite string escaping   the mother in my chest   leaves
seventeen unanswered voicemails   *no one knows how to
love you   like family*   she says   *everyone strays*

CONTENT WARNING

there is a negative space
in me, a place for what was
said, what wanted to be said
but was not said, what
was rumoured to have
been said, what could not be
said, what simply could not be

said, what will not be said but
should have been said, what
would have been said, what we
learned to say instead of
what may never be said and at
the edge of it all, what we owed
it to each other to say, but revised
it, resented it, repented for
it, who must die before it
can be said, what has to be
said, what will have to be
if we say it, when we say it

CPTSD: EMOTIONAL FLASHBACK

home. clouded recollections, neighbours silent as a blown fuse.
houses in a blank-eyed row. I'm six again when I lie here, inhaling dust
from a time I can't remember. dad smoking downstairs, the scent of rice
sharp as a mother's voice. those classroom years, every day sick
to my toenails, vomit coating the bowl. I hid my words behind the blue door
of childhood, craving the warmth of her, chest to chest, or a familiar doll

to sleep. back where I sleepwalk, rub their legs with soap, doll by doll.
I turn on every blow-dryer in the house, smell her footsteps when the fuse
burns. I never learned to bike, to open the garage door
and go. outside the window, a brick wall. a blue dream only this bedroom's dust
could tell. she likes the television for its noise. she loves me when I'm sick.
she tells me so, with no words. she forgives my father's cold rice

at the table. I count her secrets, one for each grain of rice
I swallow, two for each time she says *don't tell*, presses a wet doll
to my lips. years later, not long ago, I down the blue pills just as slow, as sick

39

with the shame of pleasure. miles of ribboned memory, a lit fuse.
my new lover kisses me on these same sheets, drowns us both in dust.
lost time buried under skin, hair, dirt. they lick my teeth. I watch the door.

time licks my hair, buries me under teeth, skin, dirt. lost, I watch the door
years later. my not-long-ago lover kisses me on sheets of rice,
skin ribboned with the pain of pleasure. memory lights miles of dust,
lifts it to my lips. I down the blue pills slow as smoke, one for every doll
I tried to swallow, two for each time she said *don't tell*, pressed a wet fuse
to my legs. I count her pores, her stories, each grain of sick

she leaves me. if I never tell him, she'll forgive my cold sick
noise. she turns on like a television. she knows my desire is a door
I'll go through. outside the dream, a window. this bedroom's fuse
blows the brick walls open. as a boy I would have learned to bike, to burn rice,
rage the whole house blue. instead, her footsteps, the blow-dried dolls
cleaner than soap. sleepwalking, I rubbed my doll legs to dust.

my whole childhood I craved a familiar warmth, to sleep on her chest. dust
coated the door. vomit on my toenails. I hid my voice behind the sick,

40

sharp as a mother's years. those classroom days, every word a rag doll
from a time I lied, lied, lied. the scent of smoke downstairs, dad closing the door.
bricked houses like a row of eyes. I go blank when I speak, when I smell rice,
when I come home. the neighbours in their windows. memory silent as a blown fuse.

the night outside hung wetly like a tongue
two moths darted into the bathroom
your lover said *call me if you start to struggle*
the doctor's number prodded
your awakeness like a door   a heavy wind
entered through   your mouth   a moth
curtained your eyes   blood-blue
you had never been more
loved   you took the pills then you woke up
your friends observed you from behind a window
three blue pills fell through the cedar decking
the doctor said *we have to call*
the police   you found two moths
singed wetly on the bulb
your friends would not let you sleep
alone   in the moth-swollen night   the wind
rustling a single door
when you woke up you were still   alive

drinking the glass with your bare hands
heavy with blue   the dead
grass howling   the odour of cinnamon toothpaste
ten pills counted from the plastic bottle
a whisper of moths   a swollen
window   it took nearly an hour
to tell   what you remembered
how your voice cracked
the wind in two   how you slept
the whole way home

BORDERLINE PERSONALITY DISORDER

301.83 (F60.3)

A pervasive **pattern** of instability of interpersonal **relationships,** self-image, and **affects,** and **marked** impulsivity, **beginning** by **early adulthood** and **present** in a variety of **contexts,** as indicated by **five** (or more) of the following:

1. **Frantic efforts** to avoid **real or imagined abandonment.** (Note: **Do not include** suicidal or self-**mutilating** behavior covered in Criterion 5.)

2. A pattern of unstable and intense interpersonal **relationships** characterized by **alternating** between **extremes** of idealization and devaluation.

3. **Identity** disturbance: markedly and persistently unstable self-image or sense of **self.**

4. **Impulsivity** in at least **two** areas that are potentially self-**damaging** (e.g. spending, **sex,** substance **abuse, reckless** driving, **binge** eating). (Note: Do not include suicidal or self-mutilating behavior covered in Criterion 5.)

5. Recurrent suicidal behavior, **gestures,** or **threats,** or self-mutilating behavior.

6. Affective instability due to a marked reactivity of **mood** (e.g., intense **episodic dysphoria,** irritability, or anxiety usually lasting a few **hours** and only rarely more than a few **days**).

7. **Chronic** feelings of **emptiness.**

8. **Inappropriate,** intense anger or difficulty controlling anger (e.g. frequent displays of **temper,** constant anger, recurrent **physical** fights).

9. **Transient, stress-**related paranoid ideation or **severe** dissociative symptoms.

BORDERLINE PERSONALITY DISORDER
301.83 (F60.3)

pattern   relationships,

affects   marked   beginning   early

adulthood   present   contexts   five

Frantic efforts   real or imagined abandonment.

Do not include   mutilating

alternating   extremes

Identity

self

two

damaging   sex   abuse   reckless

binge

gestures   threats

mood

episodic dysphoria

lasting   hours   days .

Chronic   emptiness.

Inappropriate

temper

physical

Transient stress   severe

BPD AS THE HAPPIEST I'VE EVER BEEN

pattern

of

temper

of days   to do to do

to binge

a beginning

marked by

sex and stress and effort and self

BPD AS PERSONALITY TEST

1. real or frantic
   chronic or imagined
   early or inappropriate
   adulthood or transient

         2. do the affects
            do the extremes
            do not include

3. include physical tempers
       present dysphoria
     self as mood

         4. mood as effort
           self as five or two
              or episodic

5. relationships mutilating

           6. the marked self

BPD AS LOGIC PUZZLE

by early adulthood   a self-damaging
pattern

                                      hours lasting
days

    an abandonment   context
                                      frequent   severe
frantic

                                          more mood
more   alternating

    tempers

  an identity of emptiness   adulthood of
imagined threat

BPD AS LANGUAGE-RESISTANT

I bind to bed   split bone to
bone   dis   ordered red
dirt nails   dry stone

I laid   alone   to slip
a sordid lie   I did   I bore
it all   I plied a   bird to
land   its blood   to pale

I   prey   I try   I die
I died   red   rind red

hide   red pine   red tide

SELF-DIAGNOSIS BETWEEN AFTER AND BEFORE

in the last place you look
    she is still not. he is nowhere

   to be held.
in a second, your future
    redacts, a ravenous page.

you watch a white hole

   negate the sky, surprise
your habits

   like a season.

you flip through picture frames
    of gone. steam

   on the shower door
you leaning on tomorrow

   the way trees sink
               into roofs
after a heavy storm.

you are sorry for wanting to forget.

   anyone could die at any second
   but not everyone is dying

at the same pace.
a boy is a wish.
a mother is a false memory.

a trick nesting in you
like a fibrous tumor.

everything is a defense mechanism.

eventually the dead slide
out of you like blood, brown

and beautiful.
the laundry comes out

clean. even the snow releases
your footprints, with the finality of

a mother. each wake
knocks you over with a new

kind of darkness. the boy is proud
of the tornado you are. the mother

wants to be. the sun peels open

a carcass of mornings.

someday you will be a visitor
in someone else's dreams.

was this all worth it, to know
the weight of his echo? yes, even if

you can't hold her. yes, you were worth it.
alive, you could be

happy

DIAGNOSIS

PATIENT RECORD

NAME: Velma Demerson

MEDICAL HISTORY:

born 1920, arrested May 1939 by way of the Female Refuges Act.
eating breakfast at the time. labelled incorrigible, unmanageable. some
partial reasons for the researcher to consider: rape she kept secret;
father who phoned the cops; involuntary medical experimentation,
with a baby on the way; Chinese fiancé, chosen for his consistency, his
legislated lack of family; her son, who: had severe eczema, side effect of
her forced medications; died by asthma attack at 26 while swimming.

DIAGNOSIS:

Andrew Mercer Reformatory for Women, women's prison on King
Street in Toronto. promising a homelike atmosphere, a Victorian
sensibility; that is, obedience, servility, an appetite for feminized
labour. shuttered in 1969, now the site of Lamport Stadium.

Female Refuges Act: *any parent or guardian may bring before a judge any female under the age of twenty-one years who proves unmanageable or incorrigible and the judge may proceed.... no formal information shall be requisite. the judge shall hear all cases coming before him under this section in private.*

researcher's translation: a law permitting the state to incarcerate women— no cause needed but poor, sex working, drug using, undesirable to the state in any way.

Social Hygiene Council, later the **Health League of Canada**. campaigned for sterilization of the quote-unquote feeble-minded. a discourse of vice and deviance, with all its suggestions of public threat, inheritable disease.

researcher's translation: professional front for the administration of eugenic practices. Vice President: Dr. Edna Guest, Mercer physician. how like an official history, to hide these connections. to disguise their implications. how to hope, if no one speaks a story. seeks restitution. if no one cares.

RESEARCHER: Why did you choose a Chinese man to be your lover?

VELMA DEMERSON: *God knows, the criminal tag of "exclusion" in the Chinese Immigration Act is a euphemism for "undesirable."*

What did you learn during your time at the Mercer?

The legal isolation of Chinese men from female companionship ensures that I will always be taken care of.

Did you ever regret sharing your story?

My fiancé and I are lonely people who have found each other. We share the same enemies.

Start from the beginning.

They asked: "But didn't you see any boys in high school that you liked, someone better looking?"

How will you live?

Love, now so distant, appears to me as a luxurious fantasy compared to my life of physical fear.

THE DOCTOR SEEKS SUPPORTING EVIDENCE

the bedspring whines, four creaky coils; a haunted
house after the actors have left.

her palms whisper to the pillow, wrists bent double.

the slats, lengthwise cracked, cave to his weight.

past the window's shatterproof glass, a city's anonymous dark;
penetrated by light, proof that life goes on

for someone. an empty socket

sparks. dreams
split; ghostless, until morning.

RESEARCHER: Why did you choose a Chinese man to be your lover?

VELMA DEMERSON: *He's an outcast by virtue of his race. But I am also the object of discrimination.*

What did you learn during your time at the Mercer?

It isn't a good idea to ask a girl what she's in for but everyone wants to tell the length of her sentence.

Did you ever regret sharing your story?

There's been no revolution, no conflagration whereby everything was destroyed.

Did you ever regret sharing your story?

I am being watched, more so since my escape, attempted suicide, and hysterical screaming.

Start from the beginning.

It's becoming horribly clear that my life is forfeit to a still-unknown but punitive monster— the state.

How will you live?

How could it be that a judge, knowing I'm pregnant, would refuse to allow me to marry the father of my child?

How will you live?

I am only a step away from madness. I must be careful, check every movement so there is no repetition.

A NOTE ON MOTHERS

// babies womb-grown in cells without windows

// mothers labelled vagrant; incorrigible

// mothers subjected to medical trials

// often, the administrator scrubbed confinement from birth certificates

// the gall to suppose this a blessing

// a severance from truth

// to work all day suppressing rumours of torture

// then to leave work behind when one goes home

// older children forced into domestic or farm labour

// for the term of a mother's sentence

// call it eugenics, if eugenics is what it is

// an unbearable load should not be borne alone

// through adoption, foster care

// through fighting to access the documents

// to prove the history of abuse

// to become a child of known origins

disclosure of information about an individual is permitted or required by law, without that individual's consent,

> if the custodian believes on *reasonable grounds*[1] that the disclosure is *necessary*[2] for the purpose of eliminating or reducing a *significant risk*[3] of *serious bodily harm*[4] to a *person or group of persons*[5]

---

[1] a concern that is based on more than suspicion, rumour, or speculation

[2] there is no other reasonable way
    to prevent the risk of harm to the client or others

[3] in between the extremes of low risk and certainty

[4] death or *any hurt or injury, whether physical or psychological, that interferes in a substantial way with the integrity, health or well-being of a victim*

[5] the victim(s) are identifiable or their characteristics are described specifically,

by handcuff by bedframe by sedative by last resort by wellness check by gas mask by tranquilizer by straitjacket i.e. camisole de force by forced leave unpaid of course by *step out of the car* by involuntary form by gunpoint by pen by flash photo by anaphora by electroshock by warehouse plexiglas by cinder or cement by misdiagnosis by the myth of meritocracy by rope tie by colonic by the frequency of nightmares by opium or chloral hydrate by fifty to eighty cents an hour by lobotomy by syphilis pill by manganese chloride injection by spinal drain by insulin shot by metrazol by fever cabinet by appendectomy one could call preventative by novarsam tryparsamide prazosin prozac by seroquel and ativan by food mixed with whiskey with cod-liver oil by stomach tube force-fed by passive surveillance by family meeting by story discompleted by strangers' reactions by the management of inheritance by interdiction by goodwill by meeting some basic needs but not others by coercion and cohabitation by public embarrassment by threat by soundproofed room by label at the pharmacy counter by preserving satisfactory familial functioning by boarding house by removal to the countryside by confinement in the home itself by crib-bed by waistcoat by restraining muff by censor by long-term plans corroding by any means necessary by pillow wedged at the heels of the door

PATIENT RECORD

NAME: Marie "Blanche" Wittman

MEDICAL HISTORY:

born 1859, institutionalized 1877 at La Salpêtrière by way of seizures, anger, lifetimes of trauma—her own, her father's—attempted rapes, night tremors. *perfect hysteric. model of hysteria.* star of weekly lectures and demonstrations, a medical reality show, plagued by claims of faking symptoms for attention and fame (or, the researcher considers: access to shelter, sustenance, health care, however conditional, that she needed to survive).

DIAGNOSIS:

Jean-Martin Charcot, Salpêtrière neurologist, professor, physician to the ruling class. best known for his studies on hypnosis and hysteria; refuted, ridiculed not long after his death. in his theatre, the audience surrounded Blanche with rats and snakes, invoking her by turns to act a donkey, or lady of the upper class. script of drama, salacious surprise. a presence rationed, a present displayed without history.

ETIOLOGY

hysteria: the language of limbs. to choose this is to womb the head in wilderness, to wed the suffering of your grandmothers. their survival symptoms. what state criminalizes need? claim their labels as your camouflage, but first—

A. pull the diagnosis screaming from your fists:
    1. *a chaos of symptoms*
    2. drama and deception
    3. ungovernable emotion
    4. heightened sensitivity of the skin
    5. hallucinations
    6. sleepwalking
    7. stuckness of the limbs
B. make an example out of:
    1. a medical trash can
    2. illness as fraud
    3. body as blank page
    4. a rupture between history and memory
C. consider Charcot, consultant physician to the ruling class:
    1. self-proclaimed owner of *a kind of museum of living pathology*
    2. *what grand asylum of human misery* warehoused another and another and another and another and
    3. another like you
    4. the naked fields humming
    5. each new doctor you list to your phone to never call back
    6. a rare clear-headed morning
D. the looking:
E. the listening:

D.

because burnout, again
because chronic pain
because cardboard buckling in the rain
because her face wilted when she heard the news
    her husband laying his head in another's lap
because an animal lover, Charcot experimented on human patients
because distance bungled the volume of our faces
because the car radio wound all the way up
because home became a site of confinement
        because her became our
became schizophrenia, borderline, bipolar, dissociative disorder
because the factory paid for
        our husband, our father
because assimilating to him, we relearned our dreams
because we spoke love in a language no one else could understand
            because I store my passport under the pillow
because he launched the phone at my head
because Winnicott said a mother must be merely *good*
            enough, good enough
because the ultrasound wand, slurring
because after we died our fathers never mentioned us again

        home is a palimpsest we were always revising
when our kidneys ballooned with cysts
when the factory grew so also the business
        trips, the babies disowned behind him
and ahead
    when they said *why didn't you just ask for help*

when he wrote to our grandmother calling her
another woman's name
when the police seized our friends on political charges

and they assigned to the psych unit
and they labelled *emotionally and psychologically disturbed*
and they dragged off the railway
and they cinched the restraints
and they can't
              pronounce her name, they reinvent
time as a privilege not everyone can afford, as in
              they sentenced her to years
                          and her years lose their days   and still
              she and she and she survived

because the largest psychiatric facilities are jails
because the how and where have changed, but not
                    the whether or the who
because the provincial prison dons a new and pretty coat
of paint, because the police everywhere are the same
        they don new uniforms, pretend
they're one of us

and the grandmothers are locked away
        pudding and powdered potatoes, 3.7 hours of mandated care a day
and I deity information, I stuff
                my head with facts until there is no room
for feeling
        because when the asylums
                emptied and the residential schools shuttered

    the prisons filled

and there was a time before

Mercer, before Lamport
        before encampment evictions and wooden barricades
    before broken wrists in service of
splash pads and rugby practice
                before cell flooding, bayonet swinging, my
grandmother's teacher used for target practice in a public park

    but on this side of not knowing

there is only one
arbitrary unit of seconds and the next and then the day
        after that
a sprig of thyme wilting in the bedroom window

—did you ever regret sharing your story?

in the hospital, my body becomes a map. diagnosis logs
new routes, the impulse to lie for living's sake. I won't bite back unless
asked. I'll be your perfect specimen, your choir at midnight, the
moment pain splinters into specificity: knuckle or flogger or babbling
siren. you want to know if this is the life I wanted. I don your clothes,
eat your food, indulge my vices on your dime. I bought a new corset
with money from the medical study, I married myself with my own
consent. I zipper my wedding harness. that night I hid in the garden
until dewtime, killing cigarettes in the grass. femme spectre. memory-
cyst. the scent of pink. acting works better than asking for help ever did.

—what did you learn during your time at the hospital?

it is not time that kills us, but space; the distance between diagnosis
and care, between punishment and cure. *ancestor*: someone who didn't
know better. *aftermath*: someone who passed on more than they meant
to. a cold, brick-lined face. the river between my mother's bed and
the nurses' station. every time we drive by North York General, my
reflection and my grandmother's run into each other. fistful of ginger
candies, one pair of plastic slippers, precisely arrayed. *all of my ancestors
know longing. longing is often our connecting place.* in fifteen years I will
have outlived every woman in my bloodline. it must be a mistake.

—how will you live?

music box / mechanical doll / my sickness crowns / the river in me / I
bloodless machine / I breathless organ / I belong to him / a songbird
in drag / bereft of interiority / I dog myself / I submit / to my doctor
/ body looping / helpless on repeat / this is how the river / whips its
wild into the canyon / I doll / of my body / my both wrists waxen /
I spill lemons / in the ward / my sickness leaves me / no choice / to
whom my blood submits / the metal music / blues my wrists / I bark
like a body / I spill my sickness on / my so-called saviour / my womb
cuffed / to the river / in exchange for small bribes / his name / falls out
of me / again / again / I drag lemons / over my tongue / like candy /
wild as a song / white as a doll / I birth a crown / of knives when asked
/ I answer / by exposing my neck / I betray my organs / to hear the
chorus / play for me

A NOTE ON WHITE

women who blend into the page
who, at the ballot, mark an X beside
wall, warden, who use as they have

been used. my mnemonic for all
the many forms of flight. any student
of astronomy could tell you— white

is hotter than yellow. Oh Be A Fine Girl
Kiss Me. the stars are running
a monopoly on meaning.

anything warm produces light.
I slip on the paper skins of Blanche
and Velma, feign a white tongue.

a famous academic projects my
sex tape on the lecture room wall
while the doctor dips his needle into

my heart, the mercury rising, rising.
our radiance, perfected. our refusals

inchoate. my hands absorb
more white than they reflect.

hysteria is a demure house
whose spectres are felt, not heard.

TREATMENT PLAN

TRIAGE

absentee days : old abuses surfacing in new aches : alcohol wipes
70% : besieged by worry, she consults a bot about her symptoms :
cardboard blueing in her bin : construction outside bedroom window
twelve hours a day : contact-hungry, she speedwalks alone, mashing
crosswalk buttons with her elbow : doctors, she reads, have begun
to ration care : empty hotel rooms wild across the downtown core :
encampments erupt beneath expressways : conversation fissured from
six feet away: the future, suddenly detonated : golden retrievers begin
to grey prematurely : she hews to idle streets : jangles the keys at her
lover's back door : life and life and life and : a list of events, postponed
indefinitely : live music, family reunions, surgeries : elective,
supposedly : she lathers every finger : masks pile up in waste disposal
: her clothes mountain on the floor : no going back, not anymore :
nurses divert patients to tents in the parking lot : one knuckle at a
time, labouring in soap and hot water : parents touch hands with
children through plexiglas screens : plaintive letters in mailboxes reach
past quarantine : her pre-existing conditions include swollen lungs,
having a race, a lack of self-preservation : quote : politicians said *some
people are too expensive to save* : she hears her own name : she hears
the harness tighten : skin on leather on metal on skin : the bottom
line is, Jeff Bezos makes the cost of 3,140,000 ventilators in a year :
or how many tulips from the corner store, stems sterilized in bleach
: unanswered, the phone eventually stops ringing : voicemails from
public health tell her to stay home : warehouse workers without paid
sick days fill her sanitizer order : she disinfects the light switches for
two minutes straight : if it takes X hours to unzip her mouth from her
lover's hair, what is the likelihood they will both fall sick : yesterday,
she turned her face off on Zoom : she knows her old stories : the
sacrifices they urge : down to the last word : the last letter

75

ABANDONMENT ISSUES

the year lumbers into one lunar cycle after
another meanwhile I record my daily
emotions as colour and shape in my notes app
a conveyor belt of pseudo-nostalgic sentiment

I rail against the new gentrifying
ice cream store then order
double scoops of funfetti

as a millennial I'm meant
to believe monogamy is not
the only path to relational security

the man next door gardens tulips
exclusively hundreds of throats opening
onto a concrete side alley

anemic incense on the mantelpiece
lumbar spine on the MRI
in class I collapsed like a matchstick bridge
not talented at structural integrity

a rosebush springs up
in our yard of affective value
to our landlord's wife
Bradford pears stink up the neighbourhood

by chance I always see the clock at 11:11 wishing on
what fantasy could dog my mind at the play party
what family could turn my father from the TV

spending my Saturn return in the bathtub
my ex said I reminded her of a child
meanwhile climate change piles snow on forsythia branches

I've been practicing new knots
debating natural or synthetic rope
the doctor says *we didn't think to check*
I am insecure attachment's proof of concept

selfhood submerged entirely in the internet screaming
yes and yes and yes and yes and

MANAGEMENT MODEL OF MADNESS

To confess is to answer to the name they gave you

The tree-lined, red-bricked benchmarks of normalcy

POV: you can't afford conversion therapy so you're in the backseat of a cop truck

Until 2013, the DSM considered queerness an inheritable disease

Imagined threat, lurking dormant in the collective body

The distance between disorder and distress is a myth

The distance between psych ward and doctor's office is a checkbox

This is how you come to define family: what you can't let go of, what won't let you go

Sifting through the debris of degeneracy

A decent life is a piece of furniture

Sturdy, without moveable parts

You know the state-sanctioned story—
        curtained window, two-car garage
        wellness check, bathhouse operation

A nation requires a philanthropic project

To insinuate itself into your bed

After treatment, you view your life through a grid of shatterproof glass

To normalize surveillance is a PR campaign

To which, nonetheless, you are not immune

You covet four walls, work station, administrator's approval

Your newly regulated desire, conscripted towards country

Every day, a room you can't leave confines you and you call it home

Home, in the diasporic framework, is an ethical place, not a narrative of containment.

— Rinaldo Walcott,
from *Black Like Who?: Writing Black Canada*

PATIENT RECORD

NAME: ghost chorus

MEDICAL HISTORY:

1850	Provincial Lunatic Asylum
1871	Asylum for the Insane
1905	Hospital for the Insane
1919	Ontario Hospital, Toronto
1996	Queen Street Mental Health Centre
1998	Centre for Addiction and Mental Health (CAMH)

DIAGNOSIS:

the city knows what it's seen—
beneath soil and scratch, flashback
and concrete, remnants of her and me
and you and we.

you/we, gardener of a family history.
you/we, pressed dandelion. dragonfruit·
wrist. four dollars in the wallet, daughter
at home in the wilderness of wanting.

but though the body remembers all
the blood is not always for us to tell.

ETYMOLOGY

asylum (n.)

a "without" + *sylē* or *sulon* "right of seizure"

in the 15th century, denoting a place of refuge, sanctuary

later, an inviolable shelter

so-called safe space

a benevolent institution

> "to shelter some class of persons
> suffering social, mental, or bodily
> defects"

institution (n.)

a founded thing; a thing established

a disposition, a mode of instruction, an arranged education

see also: *institutionalize (v.)*, to put into institutional life or to make
into an institution or to adjust to life
thereof, as in:

a censored letter. a last note, erased. the pencil marks
one's fingers can still read. a life composed
of edges. counting the seconds, the hours, the lost
                                        mothers, the days
how my family, even if they found me finally
on the ward, ten pills in, blue-skinned, half-

82

gone, would not know what they had done.
how even light— that moment before the door
opens, or love, that window
                    in the eye— dormant
and out of practice with dreaming, can die.

defect (n.)

a want or lack of what is essential to perfection

from *de* "down, away" + *facere* "to do, make," as in
to do away with

> what others call wholeness, genius, *brilliant*
> *imperfection*

mental (adj.)

sense of "crazy, deranged" is attested by 1927, from combinations such
as *mental patient* (1859), *mental hospital* (1891); *mental health* is attested
by 1803; *mental illness* by 1819

patient (n./adj.)

in the mid-14th century, one capable of enduring
    misfortune, suffering, provocations, etc.
    without complaint

by late 14th century (n.), a sick or injured person under medical
treatment

see also: **inpatient (n.)**, a person lodged, fed, and treated at a hospital
or infirmary, commonly used as an adjective by 1890

inmate (n.)

in the 1580s, one living in another's home

sense of "one confined to an institution" is first attested by 1834

contain (v.)

to restrain   (a mother)
to behave   (as a bent knee)
to control   (like a fist through glass)

from *com* "with, together" + *tenere* "to hold"

related usages:

to attract   (a moth)
to flatten   (like a field)
to strip   (a bed, a wing, a sheet of land)

confine (v.)

to draw a border, to shut up or contain, to restrain
   by force

related usages:

plastic pill bottle, the blue inside it
brick walls set by patients, sixteen feet high
the house, the bed from which one cannot leave
   when the mother in one's head expects of them to leave it

defect (v.)

to revolt

attest (v.)

to bear witness

home (n./v.)

to dwell, to affix, to abide, to state, to nation, to name, to target, to close, to save, to seek, to move, to go, to yellow, to ease, to stay, to say one's piece, to aim, to end, to originate, to be waiting, always, to begin

see also: **to make oneself at home**; that is, to become comfortable
   in a place one does not   (cannot)
   truly live

A HISTORY OF CONFINEMENT, DIFFERENT SITES

RESEARCHER   GHOST CHORUS

mapless / I write my way home / to a childhood of latched
mouths / walls skinned by trains and teddy bears / a madness
architecture / I had to escape

                               to explain / they said / it would bring more
                               jobs / stimulate the local economy / plant flags
                               on the loyal foreheads of police

the rules were always changing / couldn't talk or swallow or load the
dishwasher right / nights filled with new faults new injunctions

                               on intimacy / and if the prisons swelled
                               when asylums shuttered / would you call
                               that a coincidence too

in the house / without sound I reached for story / clenched barbed
wire / but it was still my fault my
fault and so I deserved / the slap

                 the pen / the intake questionnaire / the doctor / always judging bed
                               wrapped in plastic / harsh to the touch

in the soundless country / the doors never locked
I shoved my wrists / through
a window / trying to get out

                 inside the child / a thicket of mothers / slams the curtains shut

A HISTORY OF LABOUR

I polished the tracks

        I hauled the coal

I wasn't paid

        I laid the wall that closed me in

I pressed the nurse's skirt

later, she cuffed me to the headboard

        I laundered the sheets she folded me into

I dirtied my hands

the soil returned me to myself

I fitted an iron fence atop for decoration

        I signed my name to my work, five Xs and
        an accident

        sixteen feet above ground

but daily, the doctors

some sounds signify nothing

a window blocked by brick

for my own good

        for the uniform on my back

my father forgot me in a cage

he stopped visiting and nothing changed

        I took myself on a walk after dark

        I dodged the night watchman

        I slapped a baton under my bed

they gawked at us on tours

we communicated in code

        an ill-timed joke

        communal pill box

        a coil of rope

the laws changed and nothing changed

when they said we could go home

        I had no home to go

bereft of kin, we rolled our gurneys down the street

singing for our dead

I learned the languages of money, of skin

swallowed by the street's white mouth

BRICK IN THE ASYLUM WALL, 1861

my first memory was mortar. men's faces
above me, men scraping me clean with metal
and sweat. I never felt the women's hands
but heard their whispers, their yards of laundry
snapping in the wind. the gates were an afterthought.
on one side, sallow light slipped from windows
set too high to look out of. on the other
the shrill echoes of a shrinking landscape.
sometimes a skirt swished over my skin, boots
trying to climb the south buttresses. sometimes
their conversations carved the day into slices
but mostly what kept me company was quiet.
the sky open and stirring, whipping every drop
of wet from the sterile sheets they wrung to dry.
I was still new, then. I didn't even know
their names.

PARKDALE TIME-LAPSE
— from the former Mercer and asylum sites

decades of chapped hands, cold lips, concrete, case number, eye roll,
video calls to family, brownstone shaded by old oak, lake wind, thick
air, nosy neighbour, swollen joint, maggots in plastic bags, sugarcane
water, ginger soda, gossip for free, property values, exhaust off the
six-lane expressway, coins counted at the corner laundromat, the
metronome of bureaucracy, screen-printed tees, bleached sheets,
pennies littered in the gutter, garden plots behind wooden fences,
planters hung from porches like small planets, teenagers at the
playground, grandmother's scarf, grocer selling barley tea, rent strike,
siren like a white noise machine, all-night McDonald's, banquet table,
shrink-wrapped window, life distilled into the walk to work and back,
knuckles kissed by bleach, streetlamp in the hour before dawn, hand
under the hem of a lover's shirt, greeting a body like a city, an echoing
touch, mistaking the lake for an ocean, home becoming nothing more
than an idea, an idiom, impossible to translate

BRICK IN THE HERITAGE WALL, 2020

between the flower market and the old
asylum grounds, now, they lead tours.
I hear I am the landmark, the lesson.
I am often— briefly— touched. the stories
I've heard before. how the visitors mocked.
how the letters cavalierly censored
never arrived to comfort friends and spouses.
lawyers, children. how I predate even
this nation, in whose name I archive
these spectral scratches— an *X*, a name,
a date, another *X*— still, faintly, legible.
meanwhile, the walls inside the wall
become numerous, glassy, wordless.
my northwest corner proclaims
YOU'VE CHANGED in graffiti, posters
for Mad Pride, Take Back the Night.
the doctors come and go. some days
I don't echo their names even once—
the ones whose voices I've absorbed.
Francis, Sandra, Velma, Mary, May
and and and, all the innumerable others.
I keep their secrets and cannot forget.

A NOTE ON ABSENCE

where do we reside in the archive, you ask?
the ledger's memory is incomplete. mask

of white noise, of dry administrative speech
page after page, while traces of us congeal

in the corners. say queer, say femme.
say brown, Black, poor. or: one who knows home

as a permanent ache. one who desires
in all the wrong ways. long wire

soaked in salt, scraping the dead
skin from another woman's back. bed-

bound, bitten-down fingers we twist
and curl to remind each other we exist.

survival is a ritual named today, a gaze
holding history. secrecy, our place

of fugitive comfort. we, the chorus.
our paths, interrupted. ghosts, lawless.

what's left: privacy, the semblance of
a door that locks from the inside out.

the bedroom, the laboratory, the kitchen, the cage
the headline, the alleyway, the closet, the stage—

do you need our names to know we were there? living?

We begin the story again, as always, in the wake of her disappearance and with the wild hope that our efforts can return her to the world.

— Saidiya Hartman, from "Venus in Two Acts"

IN A SINGLE DAY, A WORLD CAN END

or begin again.
   centuries of soil, then only water.

      foot by foot, we plant seeds

   in the ruin of things. inside the Queen streetcar, shared
cigarette, stale

fire sealing us by the lips.

      in your heart you know. someone

        is missing.
        many ones are missing.

you, echoing in your own
        head, your hands that hold

fishgut and flood and the splintered
   handle of a hard life.

every night a bruise, a graveyard
shift between you

      and sunrise, the metal
        work makes of your body

      crunching. to you, a second
is a second   is a second.
   to us, a lily or sweetgrass or the scent of pink.

language is time

                              travel. a place to grow
                   without reserve, without levy.

             from library parking lot
                     to altar on the mantel.

there will always be more
                    of us, moving past without a sound.

LATELY, I LIVE IN HISTORY

everywhere I go I see things
no one else does anymore.

       the bus stop where my bags split
                                   six
   summers ago, plastic spitting
    mangoes
          to the sidewalk.

       the Country Style where I wrote my name
                 for the last time, before
   becoming a secret.

   beneath the scream of condos, their polished
           skins, crawling creatures in suits

I see a self
   severed, condemned to the back-then of memory.

    we left our lives incessantly.
    shelves falling off walls, tongues

disintegrating into soup.

after dinner, apple chunks in a thin bowl.
    a match sizzling in dirty water.

I misplaced
   my home. it was right—

       once, back then

back

      there

this city stranded me with my palms full of
silverware.

yesterday, I dreamed into
a corner store of ghosts. they peddled
      matches, spiced chips. unhurried

conversation, fluorescing
    like fireworks.

I am perfecting
    the technique of remembering what wants
        to be lost.

last night and ten years ago and tomorrow blustering
in my ears.

what is there to take back?

today, I dreamed of the lake
drowning me in my sleep.

after is a story
    I never imagined.

less ease, more life.

a cautionary tale. what we cannot speak

with our hands, we cannot make.

PROGRESS NOTES

Now might be a good time to rethink what a revolution can look like. Perhaps it doesn't look like a march of angry, abled bodies in the streets. Perhaps it looks something more like the world standing still because all the bodies in it are exhausted—because care has to be prioritized before it's too late.

— Johanna Hedva,
from "Get Well Soon"

A NOTE ON PRESENCE

chapstick. new inhalers. jasmine tea, looseleaf
potted bluebell on the counter. though the path is

marked by muscle, by blister, blossom
by blossom, you will forget to number

your mistakes, the sibilant missteps
between narrative and memory. bless

the fables your 姨媽 told about your mother, the basil
keeping sunlight company in the windowsill. bless

the linden earning gold its name. bless
yourself at six. at seven. even if the panic bells

clanged and you never left home. even if
the clocks melted, the blinds wouldn't

close. even if you wore your blouse
like a puppy's mouth, open to the world.

you need not be blameless
to be worthy of this blessing.

bless the ballads filled with shades of blue. bless
the ballerinas leaves make of themselves

in November. consider it possible
that you, too, are beloved. simple as that.

that for someone in this life, you are a balm. a ballast.

before word or gesture, still a scribble
in your mother's body, you chose yourself

and isn't that a blessing
too. even if you can't remember.

bless the blastocyst, bless
the silent labour of becoming. bless

a simple, honest slumber.
bless the night with no bloodlettings.

your life is not something that needs to be earned.

QUARANTINE

overnight, I stagger from one announcement to
   the next, barely daring touch except to test that

yes, I still exist— this pandemic scorns my proverb
          about waiting— I tried

to strand the sick inside— walk with elbows grazing
   the world, mouth turned away—

a couple crosses the street to avoid me— the wind crawls
   under my collar, the way I wish you would—

how far away is after— the last time we danced
   I flinched when you coughed— echinacea cones engulf

the yard from seeds I planted
   last year— the radiator bickers with the newly quiet

     night— a stranger downstairs scolds
their child daily, red sound drifting in

   from the courtyard— transit cops threaten
      empty streetcars— what isn't mine

is still not mine— all this time
   we had enough— of houses, of food—

     of friends to fill a screen or two— care, measured
in phone calls and deliveries

from a distance— the dogs don't know why

their people keep staying—

without us, the sky has more space
to breathe— I am used to rejecting what

I need— ginseng boiled into tea, a bouquet of hours
for the two of us, alone— we isolated

apart, surveying the recommendations—
as a child, I survived

on Saturdays in the stacks— stories souring
in the suburban afternoon— if I could only pour

some ancestral knowing— some dribble
of hope— from my window

my eyes stroll longer and longer, counting
dead lawns, the light drying up

inside living rooms— the same songs play
on the radio— panic wakes me

like a lover, fumbles my inhaler— the cat
turns my succulents

onto the floor, the soil
too scattered to gather—

left unread, books dream
their own dreams, uninterrupted—

of renters, revolting, and foxes
returning home— for some of us, the new normal

is old— having waited, I wait
for the day you and I can meet

hands-first— root our faces to each other's fingers
without fear—

POSSIBILITY MODEL OF MADNESS
— *after Danez Smith*

mango pits & pencil crayons & pitbulls in primary colours & the pitch
of rain hitting stone & pills flowing in the palm & limbs asweat under
a weighted blanket & tablecloth splayed out on the grass & kitchen
scissors trimming bean sprouts & cherries wet in bowls & the C of
your neck & your key in the door clicks & wild lavender you picked &
abandoned railroad tracks & holding your hand against the cops & my
index in your mouth & too humid for sleep & Frank Ocean floods the
kitchen & rice in your hair & your dad jokes your well-seasoned soups
& I list you as my emergency contact & I know you know depression's
slow drip & half-evaporated jars of water & when I had no gentleness
for me there you were & you & you & all the yous of my heart & every
child in me is learning my name

A NOTE ON MOTHERS

after I tell her I am queer, she calls me
crying, says *please don't tell your father.*

how to let this language leak through me. desire
twisted. my body reacting to what it deems dangerous.

collective noun for mothers: a static. a scream.

remember: during wartime, grandmother sewing boy-clothes
for her daughters, so they would not get raped.

after school, my fingers peel the plastic film off bak tong gou
from the chinese bakery. my mouth sweet
with steam and sugar.

remember: my mother died alone as her lungs
filled with water. this was her favourite cake.

enough, the absent mother says.

grandmothers are ties wrapped tightly
around your neck. mothers live

in hospital beds and voicemail inboxes. they tell you
they love you by holding their hands
over your eyes.

ABOLISH

what city have I woken in
tension flays the sky like a hot wind

how long will the revolution stay
is a question displacing responsibility

every hour there are choices to be made
brand name stores board up their displays

everything money can touch it sways
in the language I come from time causes   nothing

but identical seconds in which to assemble
protest kits with snacks and gauze and tape

so what if the police plant stones on every route
the dogma of peace brays from headlines

from the riotous airways of guns   rebellion
whistles underneath the Gardiner Expressway

my friends I say abolish and see your dusty stoop
with its dusty steps awaiting my arrival

I read hope in the guts of a living tree
the morning opens wet as a wound   a mouth

becomes a seam between what we pray
and what is possible

LONGING IS OUR CONNECTING PLACE

— after Stacey Park Milbern

not the ravenous day
not the mangy squirrel
not the maple tree shaking
not the nod and swerve of oncoming foot traffic
not sun dribbling into the courtyard like rotten cheddar
not vegetables softening at the back of the fridge
not clothes shedding their virality in a plastic bag by the door
not pigeons communing over dust and scraps
not the front yard foaming with coltsfoot nor the mouse
crushed on the sidewalk adjacent
not flower market Saturdays at the former asylum
not the Adjective & Adjective leisure goods establishments
not the clatter of long-legged cranes stacking luxury
across the street
not housing for those who need
but those with two maybe three
seasonal properties in Florida and Maine
not lagging Telehealth sessions
not the partial privacy of the bathroom my therapist asking why I
haven't cried in weeks
not chosen family fined for driving in one car without ID
not a large gathering only four or five
not hoarding frozen pizzas not calling the police
not cop hands evicting encampments, bending arms past their
breaking angles
just this once, everyone having everything they need
not because the first of the month looms at the window
not the audacity of landlords collecting
not the secret of an evening not shared with another
not the leftover lentils I spilled on my feet
not the new deaths daily

not the newsfeed I dissociate into
not the strangers whose profiles I scan seeking comfort
where love isn't
dopamine dispensed by the screen's red flicker

IMPACT STATEMENT

This form may be used to provide a description of
the physical or emotional harm, property damage
or economic loss suffered by you as the result of
the commission of an offence, as well as a description
of the impact of the offence on you. You may use this space
to draw a picture or write a poem or letter if it will help you
express the impact that the offence has had on you.

for years, rumours grew of a serial
killer in Toronto's Gay Village. police
continuously denied these claims; when
[   ] was arrested in January 2018
the remains of seven men were found
in planters at a home on Mallory Crescent
where he worked as a landscaper. the eighth
located in a ravine behind the property. police
continuously denied the context of this case.
until a white man disappeared, the others had
been almost forgotten. police continuously
denied who is to blame. police continuously denied
a man a man a name a man a name a man a man
a name a life a life a life a life a life a life a life a   life

in January 2019, Bruce McArthur pleaded
guilty to eight counts of first-degree murder
for the deaths of Selim Esen, Andrew Kinsman,
Majeed Kayhan, Dean Lisowick,
Soroush Mahmudi, Skandaraj Navaratnam,
Abdulbasir Faizi, and Kirushna Kanagaratnam.

I
I,I
I,I,I
I,I,I,I
I,I,I,I,I
I,I,I,I,I,I
I,I,I,I,I,I,I
I,I,I,I,I,I,I,I

I :: community of cells
I :: splintered abode
I :: system locked in fight or flight
I :: adding up on the windowsill
  :: skin, hair, pollen, soil
I :: ant gnawing holes in the kitchen wall
I :: the lens a universe looks through
I :: the lie that lives in *get home safe*
I :: shifting station

I :: a world, a world, a whole world
aching

Toronto police name eighth victim of [   ] // *Police*
'always had that feeling' a killer lurked in the Gay Village,
investigator says // *Court hears disturbing details* // *the gay*
community reacts to the [   ] *case* // *victims were*
remembered // *Toronto cop claims to be 'scapegoat' in* [
] *investigation* // *Leaside couple recounts*

                    all of our pots around
                    the house were suddenly
                    filled with beautiful flowers

they said he was by all accounts a kind and helpful man
they said no one was hunting us
they said disappearance may be a
pattern of behaviour
they said they would give the family five or six days to grieve
before pressing further
they said too complicated to translate
they said they examined the planters
they said if you look at it a different way their denial of the
evidence was an
investigative strategy
they said
they were not to blame
they said he was a white man, no one would ever imagine him
a killer
they said *we*
did everything we could
they said to the queer community after his sentence
I imagine this must feel like validation
they said they are ready to
move past this
they said the body with no identifiable owner must be
ethically cost-effectively disposed of

an *agreed statement of facts* might reveal:

eight begonias in a wet clay pot

"This is just the closure of one chapter," the Justice acknowledges,

following the sentencing,

"This court cannot give them what they want most,

to have their loved one back."
to lose the minutiae of courtroom proceedings
to reclaim the evening news as a time of monotony
to fret over ordinary things— the spit of hot oil, soiled floors,
supermarket bread gone stale
to indulge, occasionally, in dry cleaning
to excise the term *cadaver dog* from memory
to forget a casket's shine firsthand, the stunning heft of it
to call them and from their bedrooms hear an answer
to pluck their names from the news anchor's mouth, their photos from
the papers
to know
to not know
to spit on their killers
to have a home to escape and then go back to
to plant begonias, violets, tulips perhaps
to see the soil and not the sons

before, slaughter was
an abstraction. now an animal

under my eyelids. moon-faced, two
shattered
glasses, a van— lipstick

crimson as the lines I pen
to paper
to underscore

an error of tense, of
syntax. the dead
flock   my sleep—
          pigeons pecking

my cheek, teeth
falling onto my palms
like tiny tombstones.

the neighbour barks
insistently as if engaging
an enemy.
          I pray, I drape

    a mother's grief around me
the way I would a fur coat
too big for me alone.

in your place, I've imagined
    everyone I love. the Village

swells, more threat than body.
    on the shadow side of

every second, a potential killer.

       somewhere, there is a somewhere
better— no judge, no country

no need
   to hide. meet me there

   again, for the first time, our days
lined and pored

over with care, like an old
manuscript. tell me

your sentimental
       smells, the precise shade of your childhood

bedroom. the last love you grieved—
   your first wanted kiss—   in this other-
where, there will be time to ask of
such things, and ordinary

      measures of intimacy— spare keys
by the front yard planter, chamomile
  buds in bath water.

   will you   sit beside me

let our tongues
   in our skulls roll
the softest questions.

let my hands
   say your name and will you do

the same, tomorrow pouring

through a slatted
        window, your gaze

piercing bone to touch
the part of the brain that dreams—

A COMMUNITY WITNESSES

the Don River whistled us a dirge //

                                    // we reported our lovers missing

who it was we last overheard singing //

                                            // we can't recall

but the hollow note stings //

                                    // lingers in the shower walls' echo

grey, the newspaper's shadow //

                                        // our hands grazing our faces

where the city spit us out, language and ink, we lived //

                            // by headline by kindling by dusty flag, we lived

our scalps newly shaved //

                                    // bare lamps witnessing the wind

an intimacy between skin and blade //

                                    // under our eyelids, flowers undress

from petal to bone //

                                        // remind us how that lyric goes

the one about the cops and the gay bar //

                                        // then the hospital floor

then the officer demands identification //

                    // the officer, conditioned to continue smiling

at a Know Your Rights training, the facilitator teaches us
to say //

                                        // why are you arresting me?

consider how they fear our *we* //

                              // disarming the squad car radio

dirtying the words of national anthems //

                    // sifting our convictions through the mesh

of our fishnet leggings //

                    // so we practice saying we have a right to remain silent

indeed we have a right to more than remains //

                              // late at night, we train ourselves to name

our mundane children, our dogs demanding breakfast //

              // our what-ifs script a dissonance of gun, garden, uniform

inside each seed, a hammer and a melody //

                              // inside each grief, a horizon's absence

a person can survive so much living //

                                        // yes, if we must

we will go on grieving forever //

INDEX

blue, *39-42, 82, 104, 114, 141*
    bell / pill / screen / window
care, *1-150*
    as music / as resistance / as scapegoat for
consent, *35, 39-42, 55-59, 61-63, 78, 87, 139*
    with / without
eugenics, *60, 75*
    the practice / the thought process
futures, uninsured, *13-20, 29, 49, 75-76, 106-109, 113, 141*
health, the concept of, *25, 31-35, 43, 55, 63-64, 75, 78-81, 106*
intimacies, regulated, *27, 37, 57, 64, 78, 85, 93, 117*
life, rationed, *35, 55, 63, 75, 78, 114*
mommy issues, daddy issues, *30-31, 39, 49, 110*
normalcy, the notion of, *27, 31, 43, 61, 64, 71*
police, *31, 33, 35, 42, 55, 63-64, 78, 81-82, 85, 106-109, 113, 114, 117-137*
self-harm, *13-20, 42*
suicidality, *13-20, 29, 42, 139*
violence, *1-150*
    administrative / imaginative / colonial / foundational / carceral /
    domestic / legislative / medical / military / psychiatric / sexual
waiting room, *25, 31, 49, 75, 82*
white noise, *27, 71, 93*
work and its exhaustion of hours, *33, 61-70, 87, 96*
yesterday and tomorrow and the moment after that, *1-150*

UNHAUNTED

— with drummers and ghost chorus

say it to the snow.
say it to the still-hot bullet. say it
to the subway tunnel when you consider
jumping into the approaching light.
the future reeks of repetition and you are afraid
to commit. before you sleep, say it to the empty
belly of your bedroom. when you can't read
the language on your grandmother's grave
say it. in flashbacks he thrums in you, a bayonet through stone
but he left you your bones, a hook to hang each
jagged memory. your calloused throne. your first
and last home. for years you strip yourself
from photographs, how they remind you
of him and what he wanted and what he stole
veining the hallway floor in hair and mud.
say your lineage is a long braid of women, untwining
in his hands, his father's, his grandfather's.
uprooting a sapling. polishing the rifle.
ripping the cotton skin of a dress.
you bear their names like heavy robes. say it.
bind your waist in white ribbon. history's seams

are tearing. you learned violence as the sweetest love
but you learned from the wrong people.
you drop your voice into the ocean and it keeps
falling. a red roar, a battle noise, this procession of faces
you memorize by night as if loss is enough to make you love them and
it is. once, you and your mother lay alone, two hospital floors apart as
she stopped breathing. once
you sewed silence into your skin, but now the fabric is unspooling. you
are bending to the slow arc
of a drumbeat generations wide. one day at a time.
a single star, spinning. your fingers your mother's
your grandmother's. sealing dough. dabbing toothpaste off
the mirror. pulling song from a lover's wrist.
say the secret. say it to the unhaunting sky.
say your hungriest wish say *today*
I surrendered to living. say grace.
say rage. say water and elegy.
I remember. I remember. I remember you.

STAGE DIRECTIONS FOR A FUTURE GARDEN

enter drone. enter dry

blue glow. a stage, emptied of
shadow. drummers

> fade in, each facing a drum overhead.
> our trajectories slow, over-
> lapping. hollow the first strike of wood

>> against earth. hollow the din of mourning.

> how, synchronized, it yields
> to improvisation, like all grief.

at the midpoint, what's gone
grows out in both directions.

I am done with words, and my words

> are done with me. a loss the rhythm
> fills in. measures in counts of even
> four. sound precedes meaning, then

the mind follows. then draws from
the theatre a long low hum. then

>> in the wings, bells. their ringing
>> blows like smoke, or snow, and

>> following, we

till the silence of our years. sheer
mystery, that memory forms out of
shared movement. or: we have before

      and will again. by the time the shoulders
      fall, we have sung what amounts to
      a garden bed, waiting. together? enter

backbend. enter exhaustion. a few bars
linger, as if, at our most weary, we are
no longer alone. somewhere

in the soil-dark hush, a baby cries.
it reminds us of tomorrow.

an incomplete accounting of the artistic and political lineages of
these poems or, works that have cared for, challenged, catalyzed,
contradicted my own, without which this book would not exist in
roughly the order that I encountered them:

Leah Lakshmi Piepzna-Samarasinha, *Care Work* (Arsenal Pulp Press,
2018); Eli Clare, *Brilliant Imperfection: Grappling with Cure* (Duke
University Press, 2017); Liat Ben-Moshe, Chris Chapman, and Allison
C. Carey (Eds.), *Disability Incarcerated: Imprisonment and Disability
in the United States and Canada* (Palgrave Macmillan, 2014); C.D.
Wright, *One With Others* (Copper Canyon Press, 2010); Mercedes
Eng, *Prison Industrial Complex Explodes* (Talonbooks, 2017); Geoffrey
Reaume, *Remembrance of Patients Past: Life at the Toronto Hospital for
the Insane*, 1870-1940 (University of Toronto Press, 2000); Solmaz
Sharif, *Look* (Graywolf Press, 2016); Layli Long Soldier, *WHEREAS*
(Graywolf Press, 2017); Saidiya Hartman, *Wayward Lives, Beautiful
Experiments* (Penguin Random House, 2020); Fiver, *Audible Songs
from Rockwood* (Idee Fixe Records, 2017); Ejeris Dixon and Leah
Lakshmi Piepzna-Samarasinha (Eds.), *Beyond Survival: Strategies and
Stories from the Transformative Justice Movement* (AK Press, 2020);
all of TL Lewis' work on ableism, anti-Black/Indigenous racism,
and incarceration, and the ways that ableism is used to oppress both
disabled and non-disabled people; Elliott Fukui's work on disability
justice, abolition, and mad queer liberation, in particular the "Mad
World: Psychiatry, Abolition, and New Horizons" workshop and
resources on safety planning; Kai Cheng Thom, *I Hope We Choose
Love: A Trans Girl's Notes from the End of the World* (Arsenal Pulp Press,
2019); Arlo Parks, *Collapsed in Sunbeams* (Transgressive Records
Ltd. 2021); Cynthia Dewi Oka, *Fire Is Not a Country* (Northwestern
University Press, 2021); Jordan Abel, *NISHGA* (Penguin Random
House Canada, 2021); Shira Hassan and Mariame Kaba, *Fumbling*

Towards Repair: A Workbook for Community Accountability Facilitators
(AK Press, 2019); Beth Brant, *A Generous Spirit: Selected Works,*
edited by Janice Gould (Inanna Publications, 2019); Jamila Woods,
LEGACY! LEGACY! (Jagjaguwar, 2019); Daniel Sarah Karasik,
Plenitude (Book*hug Press, 2022); Bahar Orang, *Where Things Touch:
A Meditation on Beauty* (Book*hug Press, 2020); Claire Schwartz,
Civil Service (Graywolf Press, 2022); Aurora Levins Morales, *Kindling*
(Palabrera Press, 2013); Jenny Xie, *The Rupture Tense* (Graywolf Press,
2022); El Jones, *Abolitionist Intimacies* (Fernwood Publishing, 2022).

the italicized phrases in "the garden where our future grows" quote
Saidiya Hartman, from a panel discussion on the poetics of abolition;
Johanna Hedva, from "Sick Woman Theory" (*Mask Magazine*, 2016);
and Leah Lakshmi Piepzna-Samarasinha, from *Care Work*, in that order.

"money model of madness" and "management model of madness"
draw on ideas presented in Artie Vierkant and Beatrice Adler-Bolton's
Health Communism: A Surplus Manifesto (Verso, 2022), as well as the
Death Panel podcast episode featuring this book (October 20, 2022),
which helped me decode its ideas.

"glossary" references Ruth Wilson Gilmore's concept of organized
abandonment.

"CPTSD: emotional flashback #342" and "palinode" were written
in response to prompts from George Abraham's Kundiman virtual
workshop on memory and mess.

the BPD erasure suite uses text from the most recent version of the
Diagnostic and Statistical Manual of Mental Disorders, the DSM-5,
released in May 2013 (W.W. Norton & Company, 2011).

"self-diagnosis between after and before" emerged out of conversations and collaboration with artist, friend, and former co-drummer, Weijia Feng. with thanks to grief talk, tattoo sessions, and bubble tea.

the poems concerning Velma Demerson heavily reference her memoir, *Incorrigible* (WLU Press, 2004), and various government documents. the patient record in this section draws language directly from the Female Refuges Act, RSO 1950, c 134, available at: http://digitalcommons.osgoode.yorku.ca/rso/vol1950/iss2/13. the fictionalized interviews use Velma's own words from *Incorrigible*, indicated in italics.

"a note on mothers" is indebted to the ongoing advocacy, archival, and genealogical research done by the children of women formerly incarcerated at the Andrew Mercer Reformatory, including Robert Burke, Faith Lambert, and many others. I read about them at the following links: https://andrewmercerreformatory.org/ and https://aacdq.org/our-stories/andrew-mercer-reformatory-by-faith-lambert/. the phrase *a heavy load* specifically references Burke's words in this CBC article: https://www.cbc.ca/news/canada/ottawa/former-prison-baby-reflects-on-notorious-andrew-mercer-reformatory-1.5144705.

"liability culture" uses language from the College of Registered Psychotherapists of Ontario's current (2022) Code of Ethics and Professional Practice Standards for Registered Psychotherapists.

Marie "Blanche" Wittman's patient record, and sections of "etiology," are based on research from *Medical Muses: Hysteria in Nineteenth-Century Paris*, by Asti Hustvedt (WW Norton, 2011). the line *all of my ancestors know longing. longing is often our connecting place* is quoted from Stacey Park Milbern's essay "On the Ancestral Plane: Crip Hand Me Downs and the Legacy of Our Movements."

"triage" references a graphic published by Public Citizen in March 2020 comparing Jeff Bezos' fucked-up rate of wealth accumulation, measured in ventilator costs.

"patient record: ghost chorus" references historical information available on CAMH's current website. "in a single day, a world can end" and "lately, I live in history" were written collaboratively with the members of the Switch Collective (with love to, and permission from, Anna Malla, Naty Tremblay, and Sedina Fiati), during a residency at Stratford Festival's The Lab, and included in Switch's SummerWorks 2022 production, Switching Queen(s).

"etymology" draws on info from the Online Etymology Dictionary at etymonline.com, as well as a fascination with dictionary / etymology poems, the first of which I came across were probably Bhanu Kapil's Urban Dictionary definitions (in particular: "Soft Day").

"a note on absence" builds its ethical approach to writing in, against, about the archive in response to Saidiya Hartman's "Venus in Two Acts," *Small Axe*, Number 26 (Volume 12, Number 2), June 2008, p. 1-14.

"a note on mothers" borrows the line *I've been / a Canadian and done nothing to stop it* from Franny Choi in *The World Keeps Ending, and the World Goes On* (Ecco, 2022).

the long poem "impact statement" draws on news coverage from various sources such as CP24, CBC, *Xtra*, and *Toronto Star*.

"unhaunted" was written to accompany Young Park's taiko piece of the same name, composed for RAW Taiko Drummers in honour of the International Day for the Elimination of Violence against Women.

ACKNOWLEDGMENTS

nothing ever has been, or will be, created by me alone.
my gratitude and responsibility are owed immensely, immeasurably:

to all the places, people, and movements who have made my living
possible.

this book was written in Toronto/Tkaronto, on the occupied land of
the Anishinaabe, Haudenosaunee, Mississaugas of the Credit, and
Wendat peoples, Dish with One Spoon territory.

to all land and water defenders protecting their territories and
opposing settler violence.

to everyone resisting the psychiatric industrial complex and its
consequences. may all of us one day be cared for in ways we have
consented to. may all of us one day be safe, and free.

to Black feminists and abolitionists like Mariame Kaba, Angela Davis,
Ruth Wilson Gilmore, Saidiya Hartman, Dionne Brand, Canisia
Lubrin, Audre Lorde, June Jordan, El Jones, whose words I have tried
not to strip from their context, from whom I have learned everything
I know about how to dream: of a world without prisons, without cops
and psych wards and bosses, without confinement and coercion.

to the transformative justice practitioners, elders, wisdom-holders,
whether or not they name their work as such.

to the many grassroots groups and community organizations that have
offered me political homes, however temporary, and invitations into
collective imagination: Toronto Rape Crisis Centre, Queer & Trans
Asian Youth (QTAY), Disability Justice Network of Ontario, BIPOC

Grief Circles, Tkaronto/Toronto Mutual Aid, and Toronto Street Medics Collective, among others.

to the Switch Collective and collaborators, for a creative process grounded in community, shared ethic, and reciprocity: Anna Malla, Sedina Fiati, daniel jelani ellis, Naty Tremblay, Leon Tsai, Hazel Moore, and many others.

to the staff and editors of the following publications, in which some of the poems in this manuscript appeared, usually in different forms: *Academy of American Poets: Femme Futures Disabled and d/Deaf Poets Anthology; Honey Lit; Anamot Press: The Sun Isn't Out Long Enough; Black Warrior Review; VIDA Review; Tinderbox; The West Review; Spoon River Poetry Review; Briarpatch Magazine; TRACK//FOUR; TAYO: SOFT; Homology Lit.*

to the Canada Council for the Arts, Ontario Arts Council, and Toronto Arts Council for materially supporting this manuscript, even though it so ardently critiques the state.

to everyone at Brick Books, especially Nick Thran, Sonnet L'Abbé, and Alayna Munce, for risking your belief on this manuscript, before it was a book.

to all my poet-peers, my beacons, writing on madness, chronic illness and disability, including Brandon Wint, Kyla Jamieson, Conyer Clayton, Steffi Tad-y, Rob Colgate, Leah Lakshmi Piepzna-Samarasinha, Kai Cheng Thom: you make everything possible.

to the Dreaming Otherwise cohort, for reminding me of queer crip magic, for the ritual of writing together, the rigorous and joyful practices of access and ease. and to Tangled Art + Disability and Whippersnapper Gallery, in particular Sean Lee and Marina Fathalla, for supporting our gathering.

to Zoë Fay-Stindt, for an exchange of friendship, letters, and selfies that spans years and too many distances.

to Bahar Orang, Daniel Sarah Karasik, and Sanna Wani, for affirming (with such patience and kindness!) my longing for a space where revolutionary politics and poetry and puppies can meet.

to my teachers, mentors, guides, for all the real talk, before I was ready to hear it, exactly when I needed to hear it: Andrea Thompson, Danez Smith, Erica Dawson, George Abraham, Phoebe Wang, Young Park.

to my co-drummers, for giving me a space to exist in community, outside of language: Adrienne, Courtney, D, Michelle, Mila, Rae, Steph, Wy-J, Yang, Young.

to Mercedes Eng: for your books, which I have carried with me, from home to home, for years. for being so careful, and so caring, with these poems. for saying how dare they, and how can we.

to the chorus: I have written us a plural pronoun I hope is wide enough to signal solidarity without claiming identity (solidarity as in togetherness; identity as in sameness). you haunt every letter on every page. thank you.

to my friends and co-conspirators and soulmates and kin, through all the years and changes, for home: Amil, Batul, Cricket, Elizabeth, Heather, Jahari, Janika, Joe, Kris, Lorraine, Michelle, Mila, Naaila, Nikita, Noa, Wy-J.

to Ponzu and Dim Sum and Mooncake and April, for the allergies and affection.

to Myung-Sun and Boba, for greeting me at the door.

to Mom, for having my back, from before life to beyond it. to my family: this book is my way of caring for our lineages.

I wrote this part last because it terrified me, because I couldn't fathom leaving someone out. I'm sure I still have, I'm sorry, I miss you, and thank you.

how astonishing, to exist in a garden of such generosity. to get to trust you with this text. everything I give was given to me first. I believe most of all in our collective survival. thank you.

Jody Chan is a writer, drummer, community organizer, and care worker based in Toronto/Tkaronto. They are the author of *haunt* (Damaged Goods Press), *all our futures* (PANK), and *sick* (Black Lawrence Press), winner of the 2018 St. Lawrence Book Award and 2021 Trillium Award for Poetry. They are also a performing member with RAW Taiko Drummers, and an editorial board member of *Midnight Sun Magazine*.

Printed by Imprimerie Gauvin
Gatineau, Québec